KYOTO KYOTO KYOTO

*For Karen & Paul
with love!*

Chris

©2008 Gorazd Vilhar and Charlotte Anderson

Photographs by Gorazd Vilhar
Text by Charlotte Anderson
Produced by I&I Inc.
Art direction by Fumio Munakata
Book design by Katsunori Arai
Photographs edited by Charlotte Anderson

Published by IBC Publishing, Inc.
Ryoshu Kagurazaka Bldg. 9F, 29-3 Nakazato-cho
Shinjuku-ku, Tokyo 162-0804, Japan
www.ibcpub.co.jp

First Edition 2008

ISBN 978-4-925080-96-5

Printed in Japan

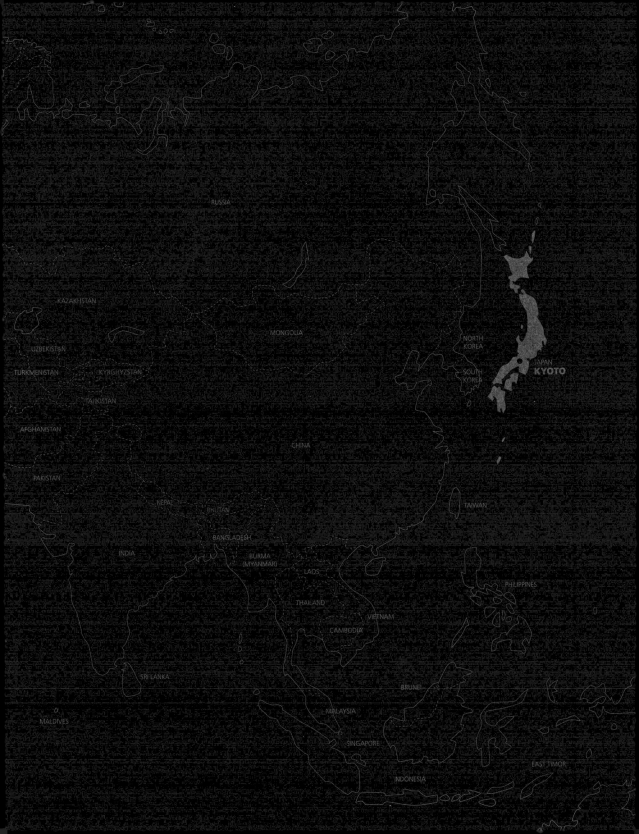

KYOTO

Gorazd Vilhar

KYOTO

Charlotte Anderson

KYOTO

I B C
PUBLISHING

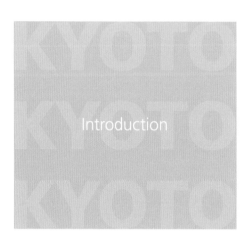

Kyoto is twelve centuries old, and the city was home to the imperial court for well over ten of them. There is no other place in all of Japan that possesses such a wealth of history, beauty, and culture. Neither is there any place so richly imbued with the spirit of Japanese tradition. Yet first impressions seem to belie that truth, for beyond the surprisingly futuristic gateway of Kyoto Station lies a busy city of crowded thoroughfares and characterless buildings spreading chock-a-block to the hills and mountains that rim the city on three sides.

Out and about along city streets, however, things begin to arrest the eye— a tiny shrine sheltering a stone bodhisattva, a venerable family crest on a shop curtain, a weathered wooden house with latticed windows. Turn the corner into a small alleyway and there, just steps beyond the hustle and bustle, can be found a gentler and more charming Kyoto. It is, in fact, a city filled with wondrous places, myriad pockets of beauty tucked away, just waiting to be found.

Geiko, as geisha are called in Kyoto, and their apprentice *maiko*, have for several centuries given Gion and other entertainment quarters a particular aura of romance, and catching a glimpse of them can be an unforgettable moment for Japanese and foreign visitors alike. As famed mistresses of the arts, these highly ornamental women serve and entertain their wealthy male clients in the secluded atmosphere of the traditional teahouses, although each decade in ever-dwindling numbers.

In 794 Emperor Kammu, Japan's fiftieth emperor, chose to relocate his capital from Nara to a geographically and geomantically agreeable spot a short distance north. Known at its inception as Heiankyo, "Capital of Peace and Tranquility," the city was modeled after the Chinese T'ang Dynasty capital of Ch'ang-an that had so impressed visiting court emissaries of the time. The ensuing Heian Era (794-1185) would give rise to one of the most refined cultures the world has ever known.

Buddhism had already been named the state religion in Nara, but, wary of religious meddling in the affairs of state, the only temples the government permitted to be built within the city walls in the earliest years were To-ji and Sai-ji, the two imperial temples charged with divine protection of the city. As Buddhist influence grew in the new capital, more temples rose up in the midst of the untamed nature that then stretched in every direction, but which has long been a part of the city itself. Through their many imperial and aristocratic benefactors, the wealth of the temples grew along with their power, allowing sacred architecture and art to flourish, many examples of which have come down to us today as national treasures.

Although Buddhism is an influential presence in Kyoto, with nearly 1,700 temples in this city of almost 1.5 million people, Shinto also accompanies

Kyoto people through their lives. Of the more than 300 Shinto shrines around the city, Fushimi Inari Taisha Shrine perhaps best reveals what Shinto means to Kyotoites. Even before the city itself was established, Inari Mountain was a site of worship of O-Inari, the deity of grains and harvest. Today, shrine visitors come not only to pray for their crops, but generally for good business and success, as well as the protection of households and companies. There are vast, mystical precincts to explore, all the way up the mountainside, through long, winding tunnels consisting of many thousands of sacred orange *torii* arches. Each arch has been purchased by a worshiper at considerable expense and placed as a votive offering to O-Inari-san.

The people of Kyoto honor the Shinto deities with a great variety of *matsuri,* or festivals, throughout the year. Two of Japan's oldest and most splendid, *Aoi Matsuri* and *Gion Matsuri,* are celebrated here with spectacular costumed processions and a plethora of related rituals, attracting a huge number of spectators from across the country. Originating over a thousand years ago, these events embody the grandeur of Kyoto's extraordinary past as they preserve city identity and pride. The faithful reenactment of these annual rites is believed to bring divine blessings to Kyoto and its inhabitants.

A remarkably large part of Kyoto is woodland, with Japanese cedar growing in the northern hills and wild bamboo forests thriving in several areas of the city. When blossoming spring cherry and red autumn maple trees come into their own, the populace and fortunate visitors are giddy with pleasure. But far more than wild nature, it is cultivated nature that has always interested the Japanese, and the people of Kyoto in particular,

for this city is home to some of the most extraordinary gardens in the world.

Already in the Heian period, garden design was a highly regarded talent among the aristocracy, and men of wealth and position vied to exhibit perfection and refinement in the gardens of their estates. Using rare rocks and well-placed plantings, they created beautiful scenes alluding to poetry, Buddhist ideals of paradise, and famous sites of natural beauty. At Kyoto Imperial Palace and several former imperial estates, the gardens continue to be nurtured and tended as the living treasures that they are. Mirror Pond, on the grounds of Kinkaku-ji, inspires visions of the elegant noble pastimes of old—pleasure boating, moon viewing, poetry parties—for this Buddhist temple, like many others in Kyoto, began its life as an aristocratic estate.

From Zen Buddhism arose a unique garden genre known as *kare sansui,* "mountains and waters without water." Inspired by evocative ink landscape paintings brought back by disciples returning from study with Chinese Zen masters, highly stylized dry landscapes representing a spiritual cosmos were created from sand, gravel, and rocks, as ideal places for meditative contemplation. Today the most famous of these gardens are crowded with busloads of sightseers, while others less known remain quiet havens of solitude and spirituality.

And so it is that this city has come to be guardian of a huge legacy of history and culture. For the visitor, Kyoto is a city of details, with much of its beauty found tucked among dreary buildings, safeguarded behind walls, shaded by screens. Yet, hidden or not, so great is the wealth of this ancient place, a lifetime is hardly enough to see it all.

Viewed from Sai-mon, the 8-pillared West Gate of
Kiyomizu Temple, Kyoto spreads westward toward the
Nishiyama Mountains. The temple was founded in the
late eighth century and is named for the "clear water"
that flows from a hillside spring nearby.

KYOTO
KYOTO The City
KYOTO

This popular landmark, Kyoto Tower, built in 1964, stands opposite Kyoto Station. At a height of 131 meters, with an observation deck situated at 100 meters, it provides a panoramic view over city rooftops to the nearby mountains.

The mirror-glass facade of Isetan Department Store catches the reflection of a billboard advertising *sake* on the roof of a neighboring building. This 13-floor emporium is part of the monumental Kyoto Station complex.

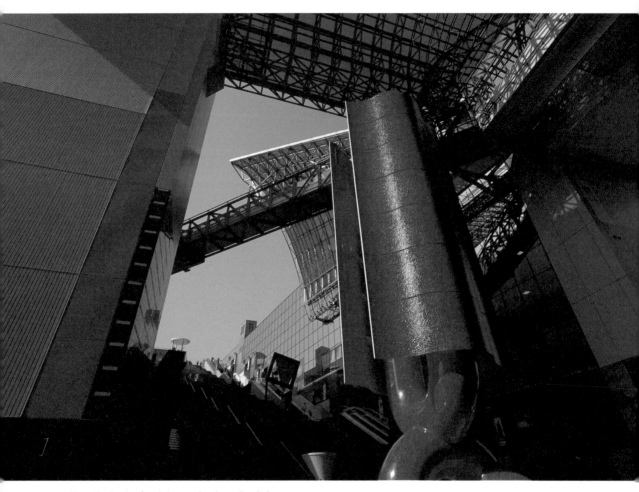

Kyoto Station is a futuristic, grand-scale steel-and-glass
structure designed by renowned Japanese architect
Hiroshi Hara. It opened in 1997 to commemorate the
1,200th anniversary of the city.

Inside Kyoto Station, bilingual signage on navigation columns guides passengers and visitors to train gates, taxis, buses, and a variety of services, as well as in-station shopping malls and a hotel.

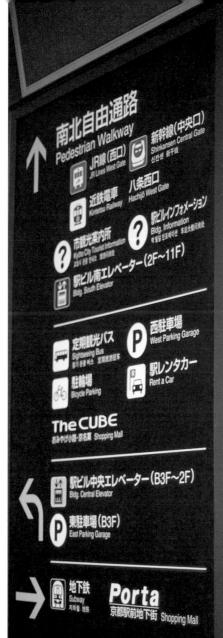

↑ 南北自由通路
Pedestrian Walkway

JR線（西口）
JR Lines West Gate

新幹線（中央口）
Shinkansen Central Gate 신간선 新干线

近鉄電車
Kintetsu Railway

八条西口
Hachijo West Gate

市観光案内所
Kyoto City Tourist Information

駅ビルインフォメーション
Bldg. Information

駅ビル南エレベーター（2F～11F）
Bldg. South Elevator

定期観光バス
Sightseeing Bus

西駐車場
West Parking Garage

駐輪場
Bicycle Parking

駅レンタカー
Rent a Car

The CUBE
おみやげ小路・京名菓 Shopping Mall

← 駅ビル中央エレベーター（B3F～2F）
Bldg. Central Elevator

東駐車場（B3F）
East Parking Garage

→ 地下鉄
Subway 지하철 地铁

Porta
京都駅前地下街 Shopping Mall

↑ JR線（中央口）
JR Lines Central Gate
新幹線のりかえ口

鉄道案内所
Railway Information

きっぷうりば
Tickets

→ 南北自由通路
Pedestrian Walkway

JR線（西口）
JR Lines West Gate

新幹線（中央口）
Shinkansen Central Gate 신간선 新干线

近鉄電車
Kintetsu Railway

八条西口
Hachijo West Gate

市観光案内所
Kyoto City Tourist Information

駅ビルインフォメーション
Bldg. Information

駅ビル南エレベーター（2F～11F）
Bldg. South Elevator

定期観光バス
Sightseeing Bus

西駐車場
West Parking Garage

駐輪場
Bicycle Parking

駅レンタカー
Rent a Car

The CUBE
おみやげ小路・京名菓 Shopping Mall

← JR京都忘れ物センター
Lost & Found

タクシー
TAXI Taxi

駅ビル東エレベーター（1F～7F）
Bldg. East Elevator

交番
KOBAN

東駐輪場
East Bicycle Parking

ホテルグランヴィア京都
HOTEL GRANVIA KYOTO

京都劇場
KYOTO THEATER

From the vast, cavern-like Kyoto Station atrium, towering banks of escalators rise to the viewing terrace atop the building. They also allow egress at several levels, leading to cafes, restaurants, a tourist information center, and a huge department store.

The Chrysanthemum Gate at To-ji Temple is graced by
the imperial flower motif within its latticework design.
The temple dates from 796, when it was one of two
important temples established to spiritually protect the
new capital. To-ji is a UNESCO World Heritage Site.

In the heat of summer, a Kyotoite elegantly wrapped in kimono and obi shades herself with a parasol. Traditional dress can be seen more often today in this historical city than elsewhere in Japan.

A traditional *machiya*-style building houses a Gion teahouse. Reed blinds screen the upper-floor windows, while a noren curtain hangs at the entrance. The noren bears an ivy crest, a historically popular motif in the geisha quarters.

Hojobashi Bridge spans the pond at Shinsen-en, the Divine Spring Garden, which has existed in the heart of the city since around the year 800. Fallen to ruin and restored twice, the garden today is only about one-tenth its original size.

At Ima Kumano Jinja Shrine, *ema* prayer plaques bear the image of the three-legged crow that, in prehistoric times, is said to have led the mythical Jimmu to Yamato, where he became Japan's first emperor.

The east gate of Nijo Castle is constructed of massive wood with iron spikes, some ornamented with breast-shaped fittings called *chichikanagu*. Built in the early seventeenth century for Tokugawa Ieyasu, the castle served as the residence for the two-and-a-half-century succession of Tokugawa shoguns whenever they were in Kyoto from their main seat in Edo, old Tokyo.

Maiko, apprentice geisha, make their way around Gion Shimbashi on one of two days each year when they and their elder geisha sisters make formal visits to their employers at teahouses and traditional restaurants to thank them for their patronage.

The tile roof of Myoman-ji Temple, with its ridge ornamentation, gleams silver in the sun. Fired clay tiles were first introduced to Japan in the sixth century from China, along with techniques of temple construction.

さよみず人形

Representations of *gosho ningyo*, imperial palace dolls, decorate an old doll shop in the Kiyomizu Temple neighborhood. Styled like chubby, happy-faced babies, these dolls originated in the early seventeenth century as charming gifts for palace visitors.

An artful path of old stones leads to the entrance of Narita, a 200-year-old shop that specializes in the making of Japanese-style pickles from *suguki-na,* turnip leaves.

Koi brighten a small stream alongside a traditional Kyoto tea-and-sweets parlor in the Higashiyama district. Such carp are prized for their ornamental appearance and can be highly collectible and sometimes extremely valuable.

A mirror and a *magatama* curved "jewel," representations
of two of the three objects that comprise the sacred
imperial regalia symbolizing the Emperor's legitimacy,
hang on one side of the entrance to Heian Shrine's main
hall during its annual festival. On the other side, not seen
here, is the third object, a sword.

The Zen temple Myoshin-ji was founded in 1337 by the
retired emperor Hanazono. The large main hall, with its
massive roof, dominates the precincts that encompass
more than fifty sub-temples.

A Kyoto matron wears an obi with a design of highly stylized peacock feathers, tied in the *o-taiko,* or drum, style. Many obi are highly decorative, and they can be several times more costly than the already expensive kimono.

Maiko out making their summer courtesy calls along the streets of the geisha quarters attract a great deal of attention from tourists and photographers. Beautiful in their formal dress, these apprentice geisha tie their luxurious obi in a unique way, with both ends left dangling attractively.

Pedestrians and vehicles cross the Kamo River via the often congested Shijo-Kawaramachi Bridge. The neighborhood surrounding the intersection of the streets of those names is a popular area for shopping, dining, and entertainment.

An illustrated map of
Kyoto is reproduced
on traditional Japanese
washi paper. This
souvenir item shows
the rectilinear layout of
the city, which was
patterned after the
ancient Chinese
T'ang dynasty capital,
Chang'an.

An antique ukiyo-e woodblock print by the celebrated
artist Hiroshige depicts geisha in attendance at an Edo-
era summer party along the banks of the Kamo River. Still
today, the city's riverside restaurants customarily open
yuka, outdoor dining terraces, during the sultry summer
months.

A vermilion-red *torii*, a Shinto gate marking entry to a sacred place, stands at the entrance to Iwato Ochiba Shrine. In late autumn, the gingko trees turn golden and the grounds are carpeted with fallen leaves.

The face of a *maiko* is
obscured by shadow and
her *hana-kanzashi*,
a dangling hair ornament
handmade of delicate
silk. The autumn maple
leaves correspond to the
month of November, as
each month of the year
has its own traditional
motif and colors.

A boldly crested *noren* hangs in front of the entrance to the teahouse Yuranosuke, which takes its name from the main hero of a popular kabuki classic about loyalty and revenge, inspired by an actual incident of the early eighteenth century, when his master was unfairly forced to commit ritual suicide.

Wooden *geta* stand at the entrance to the famous Ichiriki teahouse, for guests and staff to wear in the courtyard. Although the nearby Yuranosuke teahouse bears the name of the eponymous kabuki hero, in fact it was here where he made his show of a dissolute life, all the while quietly plotting eventual retribution with his fellow samurai against their late master's nemesis.

A couple enjoys a meal at the popular Kyouen "rest complex" above Sanjo Keihan Station in Higashiyama, where cafes, restaurants, and traditional design shops surround a courtyard garden.

Seeking to escape the summer heat, Kyotoites often
come to the northern hills to dine at restaurants where
terraced platforms called *kawa-doko* are built over
the cascading Kibune River. The surrounding nature is
emphasized in their cuisine, which features freshly caught
river fish and wild vegetables of the season.

A tray of grilled sparrows is displayed in front of a nostalgic restaurant near the gate of Fushimi Inari Shrine. Since ancient times, local farmers have been turning the sparrows and quails that were the bane of their rice fields into a bony but tasty portable snack.

The vegetarian cuisine called *shojin ryori* follows traditional Buddhist proscriptions against eating meat and fish, with roots in the ascetic practices of Zen Buddhism. Through the centuries it has developed into a highly creative and often very sophisticated cuisine.

On the occasion of a
tea ceremony at
Kitano Tenmangu
Shrine during plum
blossom season, a *maiko*
has decorated her hair
with a profusion of silk
plum blossoms.
The ceremony honors
Sugawara-no Michizane,
a ninth-century scholar
who is worshiped
there as a deity, and
for whom that flower
was a favorite.

A shop filled with fans of every type occupies a spot along a popular temple sightseeing route. The first flat fans were introduced to Japan from China in the eighth century, but folding fans were a Japanese invention.

The banks of the Kamo River in Pontocho are a popular dating and strolling spot, particularly on hot summer evenings. Scores of restaurants lining the river open their terraces for al fresco dining by the soft glow of candles and paper lanterns.

Senbazuru, clusters of a thousand *origami* cranes, hang at a shrine, where they have been left as a votive offering. Cranes are symbolic of longevity and of celebration, so they often accompany worshipers' prayers for health or for success.

Masks representing a deity called Madara and its Nio guardians are displayed beneath the eaves at Koryu-ji Temple. They are sold as talismans against robbery and other dangers at a ceremony that has been held there for a thousand years.

Young people wade in Arashiyama's Katsura River on a hot summer day. This waterway originates as the Hozu River in the mountains northwest of Kyoto. As it flows through the city, the name changes to Oi, and beyond the nearby Togetsukyo Bridge it becomes Katsura.

A woman strolls Sanneizaka at the foot of the Higashiyama eastern mountains. Part of the *monzen-machi* "gate town" area that lies between Yasaka Shrine and Kiyomizu Temple, this old neighborhood of traditional shops and houses is part of the Sanneizaka Preservation District.

The Ceremonial Hall of State stands within the walls of
Kyoto Gosho, the Imperial Palace. The palace was home to
the emperor and his family until the imperial seat was moved
to Tokyo in 1869.

The *bussoku-seki* standing beneath the eaves of Kiyomizu Temple bears representative imprints of the Buddha's feet, embellished with symbols of the Buddhist faith. Prayers offered at this stone are said to extinguish all sins.

A silk brocade banner bearing a golden *aoi* leaf crest hangs at Kamigamo Shrine during the celebration of *Aoi Matsuri*. *Aoi* is often translated as "hollyhock", but it is actually a kind of wild ginger.

At Fushimi Inari Taisha Shrine, long tunnels of thousands of *torii* wind their way up Fushimi Mountain. Each one of these sacred Shinto gates has been bought by a worshiper and given in plea or gratitude as an offering to the deity of grains and commerce.

A Kyoto *tatami* shop displays their creative coasters and table mats, made from straw and bound with colorful brocade, just like the floor mats that they have long crafted for traditional Japanese rooms.

A *maiko* passes through the architecturally preserved zone of Gion Shimbashi, an area with numerous traditional restaurants and teahouses. On the stone streets her wooden *okobo* clogs make a "pokka-pokka" sound, which gave rise to the footwear's alternate name, *pokkuri*.

Byodo-in Temple, which dates back nearly a thousand years, stands amid spring cherry blossoms at the edge of A-ji Ike, a pond designed in the shape of "A", the first letter of the Sanskrit alphabet. Originally the site of the country villa of a powerful Heian court nobleman, it was turned into a Buddhist temple by his son after his death.

At the height of the cherry blossom season, the flowering grove at Kiyomizu Temple is illuminated for night viewing. One of Kyoto's oldest temples, it was founded in the late eighth century. The main hall, a National Treasure, has a terrace supported by an interlocking system of wooden pillars and beams assembled without nails.

The Phoenix Hall of Byodo-in Temple houses a magnificent
Amida Buddha statue, surrounded by an array of bodhisattvas
floating on clouds. Carved by the master sculptor Jocho nearly
a thousand years ago, the statue is a National Treasure.

The carved and ornamented Chinese-style gate, Karamon, leads to the Ninomaru Palace and gardens within the Nijo Castle complex. It is a treasure of the Azuchi-Momoyama period of the late sixteenth century when the Japanese arts flourished.

A wall at Tenryu-ji Temple in Arashiyama is handsomely composed of a variety of old roof tiles, including a circular *mon-gawara* decorated with a crest. Tenryu-ji is a Zen temple, and such reuse of materials to avoid wastefulness is exemplary of Zen philosophy.

A sheer windblown shop curtain casts its shadow over a paper lantern on a Gion street. The lantern bears the "melon" crest, which has a long history in Japan since it was adopted from China in the sixth century.

A straw *shimenawa* demarcates the sacred Shinto precincts of Heian Jingu Shrine. Built in 1895 to commemorate Kyoto's 1,100th anniversary, the shrine possesses the architectural style of the Heian period, the founding era of the city. The spirits of Kyoto's first and last emperors, Kammu and Komei, are enshrined there.

A neighborhood cat has found a tranquil spot amid the busy precincts of Yasaka Shrine. Situated at the foot of Higashiyama, Yasaka has been one of the most popular religious sites in Kyoto since at least the tenth century, when no visit to Gion was complete without a prayer offered there.

The Gate of the Three Luminaries, named for the sun, moon, and stars, leads to Kitano Tenmangu Shrine. A gilded lantern bears the plum blossom crest in honor of ninth-century scholar Sugawara-no Michizane, whose spirit is enshrined there as the deity Tenjin, and who is said to have greatly admired that flower during his lifetime.

Split bamboo forms a decorative protector at the base of a traditional building. The so-called *inu-yarai* protects the wall from soiling by *inu* (dogs) and from splashing water and mud, and also serves as a screen for unsightly utilities.

The *shimada-mage,* a women's hairstyle of the seventeenth century, is depicted on traditional *ema* prayer plaques at Yasui Kompira-gu Shrine. An ema museum on the shrine grounds holds a large, historic collection of these appealing religious artifacts.

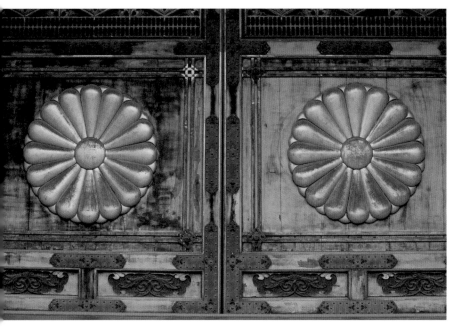

Chrysanthemum crests mark the Imperial Envoy Gate at Higashi Hongan-ji, signifying a traditional relationship between that Buddhist temple and the Imperial House. In the past, and even now, its chief priest customarily marries an imperial relative.

Kodai-ji Temple was established in 1605 as a memorial to Toyotomi Hideyoshi, by his widow. The splendid golden ceiling in the Hall of Worship was transferred there from the famous warlord's private ship.

The Koyasu Pagoda stands in the forested precincts of Kiyomizu Temple in the foothills of Higashiyama. It is believed that pregnant women who come to this pagoda to pray to the Koyasu Kannon are assured of an easy childbirth.

The Founder's Hall of
Kodai-ji Temple
nestles in beautifully
landscaped grounds
in the eastern hills.
This Zen temple was
built in the early
seventeenth century as
a memorial to warlord
Toyotomi Hideyoshi.

A *yakatabune* pleasure boat is poled across the Oi River
in Arashiyama, an area of western Kyoto that has been
a popular place of leisure for many centuries. At twilight
the scene can take on the atmosphere of an old ukiyo-e
woodblock print.

A stone statue of Senju Kannon, the so-called "thousand-armed" Buddhist goddess of mercy, stands on a small islet in Hirosawa Pond. Her many arms symbolize the belief that she is able to come to the aid of all who need her.

A fisherman casts his net into the Kamo River, just below
Shijo Bridge in the heart of the city. The river is named for
the wild ducks that still frequent its waters, particularly
along its northern reaches.

Togetsukyo, the Moon-Crossing Bridge, spans the tree-lined shore of the Katsura River in Arashiyama. The bridge, although rebuilt in the last century, has a history dating back to Heian times, when this area was a place of leisure for the aristocracy.

A statue of the white fox messenger to Inari-san, the deity of grains and commerce, stands in front of the small Inari-sha Shrine, within the extensive grounds of Kitano Tenmangu Shrine.

At a Shinto shrine, an *o-mikuji* is tied to a bare winter branch of a weeping cherry tree. Drawing such printed fortunes by lot has been a popular custom of worshipers for centuries, and they often leave them behind in this way for the attention of the deities.

A pumpkin is one of various seasonally changing offerings to Amida Buddha at Joruri-ji Temple. The splendid gilded statue stands at the center of a group of nine Buddhas in the Amida Hall, and together they comprise a National Treasure.

Golden-orange maple leaves accent the stylized *kato-mado* "flame windows" at Konkai Komyo-ji Temple. Kyoto is much beloved for its many maple trees, which attract a multitude of sightseers each November when they take on autumn colors.

Throughout Fushimi Inari Taisha Shrine's vast precincts stand innumerable mystical sites of worship centered on Inari-san. Newly harvested rice stalks and burning candles are offered to this deity of grains and commerce in front of statues of its fox messengers.

Diners are on view at a popular restaurant venue in the Pontocho entertainment district, yet they also have their own view down to Shijo Street and the Kamo River from the building's position next to Shijo Bridge.

Kinkaku-ji, Temple of the Golden Pavilion, built in the
thirteenth century as an aristocratic villa, was turned into
a Zen temple in the fourteenth century in accordance
with the wishes of its last owner, retired *shogun* Ashikaga
Yoshimitsu. It was destroyed by arson in 1950, but was
replaced soon after by a reproduction, faithful in every
way but with more extravagant gilding.

Pigeons, messengers to the deity of Miyake Hachiman-gu Shrine, are the decorative motif on its opulent *mikoshi* portable shrine. The deity, who is believed to calm temperamental children, is popularly known as Mushi-Hachiman, or "Worm-Hachiman," for it was once believed that the cause of such behavior was a worm inside the child.

A glowing stone lantern is framed by maple trees in the garden of Enko-ji Temple. Every autumn the temple opens for night viewing of seasonal foliage, a time-honored pleasure of Kyoto life.

In Gion, a round *yoshino-mado* window graces the facade of an old *machiya* townhouse, along with a classic rectangular window. Soft, golden light attractively filters through the inner *shoji* screens made of *washi* paper.

Festivals

Women in lavish costumes representative of court
attendants of the Heian period (794-1185) take part in
the *Aoi Matsuri* procession. The oldest festival in Japan,
dating from even before the city's founding, it is a
reenactment of an ancient imperial procession to petition
the gods to stop inundating rains.

During a preliminary ritual to *Aoi Matsuri,* the festival princess, called Saiodai, ritually purifies her hands in the Mitarashi Stream that flows through the grounds of Kamigamo Shrine. Once an unmarried daughter of the emperor sent to serve the gods for life as a priestess, Saiodai is now a brief honorary role filled by a cultured daughter of the city.

Apprentice geisha called *maiko* perform the Sparrow
Dance during the celebration of *Gion Matsuri*. Based on
a famous old folk tale, the dance illustrates the virtue of
repaying one's obligations.

In appeal for a safe growing season and eventual abundant harvest, Matsuno-o Taisha Shrine celebrates *Onda-Sai* each July. Sanctified girls carry sheaves of young rice plants in procession from the shrine field to the main hall, where the plants are ceremonially placed on an offering tray and brought before the altar by shrine maidens.

A group of musicians rides atop one of thirty-two magnificently decorated floats in the age-old *Gion Matsuri* procession. Dating from 869, this festival, celebrated every July, has become the veritable symbol of the city of Kyoto.

Lady Fujiwara, a thirteenth-century poet, is immortalized at *Jidai Matsuri,* the Festival of the Ages. She is represented in the style of traveling clothes she might have worn on her trip to Kamakura, when she wrote the travel diary for which she is known.

Each summer in early July, geisha and *maiko* of the Gion Kobu *hanamachi* community gather at Yasaka Shrine to pray for health, prosperity and performance skills, in a ceremony called *Miyabi-kai*. On that day they all, from the youngest to the oldest, dress simply in matching summer *yukata*.

Sacred children called *chigo,* who have undergone
purification and are the embodiment of the deities during
Gion Matsuri, are led to Yasaka Jinja Shrine to pray for a
safe and successful festival.

Imperial messengers in ceremonial garb bear traditional ancient offerings—boxes of linen and silk cloth, and silk and cotton thread—from the emperor to Shimogamo Jinja Shrine, during Aoi Matsuri.

Every year when the cherry trees bloom in Kyoto, Yoshino Tayu, a renowned courtesan of the seventeenth century, is honored with a commemorative tea ceremony performed by geisha and *maiko*. Called Yoshino Tayu Hana Kuyo, it is held outdoors in the quiet surroundings of Josho-ji Temple, the tayu's burial place.

The honorary princess of *Aoi Matsuri*, the Saiodai, walks to her palanquin at the start of the festival procession. She is dressed in splendid garments of silk brocade and wears her hair in the ancient way of Heian court women.

Paper tubes of unpolished rice and budding plum branches are presented as offerings at the *Baika-Sai* festival at Kitano Tenmangu Shrine. This Plum Blossom Festival is celebrated each February, when the shrine's orchard is in bloom.

Yoshino Tayu, a high-ranked courtesan of the seventeenth century, celebrated for her great beauty and wit, is immortalized at *Jidai Matsuri*, the Festival of the Ages.

Wearing traditional festive finery of kimono and ornate *pokkuri* clogs, a child visits a Shinto shrine to receive blessings for health and happiness during *Shichi-Go-San,* the Seven-Five-Three Festival

At *Aoi Matsuri,* a female rider representing a Heian-era guard to the Saiodai princess wears brocade-cuffed, lacquered leather boots called *kanokutsu,* designed after the onetime footgear of Mongolian riders.

Beautiful and brave Tomoe Gozen, the legendary twelfth-century warrior and reputed concubine to General Minamoto Yoshinaka, is portrayed on horseback in *Jidai Matsuri,* the Festival of the Ages.

O-mikuji, luck-of-the-draw printed fortunes, fill the branches of a tree at Heian Jingu Shrine. For the occasion of their spring festival, which occurs during cherry blossom season, the paper used is a seasonal pink instead of the customary white.

A skirted paper umbrella bearing the triple *tomoe* crest stands atop a festival float in the *Yama-Boko Junko* parade held during the monthlong *Gion Matsuri*. Over its more than eleven centuries of history, the parade has grown in size and grandeur to comprise thirty-two magnificent floats.

Worn and broken bamboo tea whisks are honored with a requiem, the *Chasen Kuyo,* celebrated by the priests of Kosho-ji Temple and followers of *sado,* the art of the tea ceremony. During the ritual, the old whisks are praised for their usefulness, thanked for their long and faithful service, and duly burned.

The princess-priestess of
Aoi Matsuri, crowned
with a golden imperial
headdress, wears a replica
of the magnificent
Heian-period *junihitoe,*
twelve layers of colorful
silk robes weighing over
thirty pounds.

Women in the costumes and hairstyles of early periods
of Japanese history take part in the procession at *Kushi
Matsuri*, the Comb Festival, at Yasui Kompira-gu Shrine.
Eras from the Kofun or Tumulus period (300-710 A.D.) up
to today are represented.

Priest-dancers and priest-musicians, respectively dressed in vermilion and deep magenta ceremonial robes, await the arrival of the *Aoi Matsuri* procession at the gate of Shimogamo Jinja Shrine.

Shrine maidens called *miko* perform a dedicatory dance at the annual *Funaoka Taisai* at Kenkun Jinja Shrine. The celebration commemorates Oda Nobunaga, the sixteenth-century *daimyo* and major figure from Japan's history whose spirit is enshrined there.

Vivid crimson lips and white makeup are the trademarks of the stylized beauty of a *maiko*, captured in detail as she prepares to perform a Shinto offertory dance during *Gion Matsuri*.

The ceremonial footwear of the *Saiodai* is left on the steps when she enters the shrine building during the *Aoi Matsuri* rituals. The clogs, called *asa-gutsu,* are made of padded red and white silk.

Young women in the roles of Heian-period court ladies wear brocade robes in an array of harmonious colors and patterns. Their hair mimics the style of a thousand years ago, when fashionable aristocratic women let their hair grow as long as possible.

The *chigo*, the sanctified child of *Gion Matsuri*, embodies the spirit of the shrine deity during the festival. He will ride at the head of the lead float in the festival procession, and his ritual act of perfectly severing a sacred rope is believed to help ensure divine blessings for Kyoto in the coming year.

KYOTO
KYOTO
KYOTO

Gardens

The pond and plantings of the stroll garden at Katsura Rikyu take on deep jewel tones at twilight. Built in the seventeenth century, this imperial villa is considered the epitome of Japanese architectural and garden arts.

A bamboo-lattice window looks out on the grounds
of Gio-ji in Arashiyama, named for a twelfth-century
shirabyoshi dancer Gio, who was in love with the famous
leader of a warring clan. When he eventually spurned
her, she retired to this Buddhist temple to live out her
days as a nun.

Stepping stones lead into a bamboo grove at Rakusai Bamboo Park, where more than a hundred kinds of bamboo from around Japan grow in a protected environment. More than half of Kyoto is forest land, and wild bamboo forests still exist in several parts of the city.

At Ginkaku-ji Temple, a sand mound stands at the edge of the dry landscape garden. Shaped into a perfect truncated cone, the mound is often likened to Mount Fuji, and its circular top to the full moon. The "Sea of Silver Sand" extending from the mound was named for its silvery appearance in the moonlight. It can also be viewed from behind the open paper *shoji* of an arched *kato-mado* temple window.

A Chinese-style corridor bridge spans a pond inlet at Shosei-en Garden, belonging to but detached from Higashi Hongan-ji Temple. The present garden dates from the mid-seventeenth century, although a garden has existed at this site since the ninth century.

From a shaded bower at Taizo-in Temple, the view opens onto a stream gently flowing over a three-tiered waterfall into a pond, surrounded by extensive rockery and plantings. The garden was designed by Nakane Kinsaku in 1963.

Remnants of Heian-era garden design can still be seen
at Hokongo-in Temple. Poets of that venerable age
found this garden so inspiring that they immortalized it
in poems that have been passed down to the present in
imperial poetry anthologies.

Cherry trees bloom along the edge of Osawa Pond in the compound of Daikaku-ji Temple. Dating from the early ninth century, the pond was originally the centerpiece of Emperor Saga's imperial retreat.

Smooth beach stones, said to number 111,000, pave the shore of the South Pond of the Sento Imperial Palace gardens. The stones were originally a gift for the garden from a provincial *daimyo,* and had been presented at the palace, each one individually wrapped in silk.

A heron perches on a stone slab bridge on the grounds of Shugaku-in Imperial Villa. The extensive naturalistic gardens and undisturbed nature beyond its perimeter, provide habitats for many kinds of wildlife.

The idyllic garden of Renge-ji comes into its own during the season of changing autumn colors called *koyo*. The pond, fed by a mountain stream, is accentuated by a handsome collection of rocks.

The modernist dry landscape garden of Ryogin-an Temple, designed by garden master Mirei Shigemori, features stones set into two shades of gravel, and a bamboo fence patterned with stylized thunder clouds.

The rocks in the garden of Ikkyu-ji, a Zen temple in
Yamashiro, are said to symbolize the sixteen disciples of
Buddha amid a mountain landscape. Although the clipped
hedge marks the boundary, the "borrowed scenery" of
the foliage beyond adds depth to this Edo-period garden.

A bamboo ladle lies atop an old lichen- and moss-covered stone water basin, at the edge of the pond at Renge-ji Temple. This garden, with its profusion of Japanese maple trees, is a popular place to view autumn foliage.

In the stroll garden at Ginkaku-ji Temple, visitors pausing to admire the hillside "Moon-washing Spring" customarily cast a coin upon a nearby rock and offer a prayer or make a wish.

Saiho-ji Temple is popularly known as *Koke-dera,* the "Moss Temple," for its exceptional garden carpeted in more than a hundred kinds of moss. In its shaded precincts, even the light is green, as it filters through the leafy canopy overhead.

In the raked sand garden at Tofuku-ji Temple, a single spiral pattern, representing one of the eight rough seas expressed therein, is caught in the last rays of the afternoon sun.

The "Garden of Grandeur" spreads in front of the abbot's quarters at Kennin-ji, the city's oldest Zen temple, founded in 1202. This meditation garden dates from 1940, when those quarters themselves underwent restoration.

Flat river stones laid in an overlapping pattern create the
remarkable impression of a flowing stream, in the garden
at Shinnyo-in Temple constructed in the sixteenth century.

A stone pagoda surrounded by rocks, moss, and trimmed bushes stands in the sylvan setting of Sanzen-in Temple in Kyoto's northern hills. The garden, called *Shuhekien,* is viewed from the temple's traditional *shoin* study hall.

The Crouching Dragon Bridge crosses Blue Dragon Pond at Heian Shrine. This unusual stepping stone bridge is composed of foundation pillars salvaged from the old sixteenth-century Sanjo and Gojo Bridges when they were later rebuilt.

A caretaker tending the Sento Imperial Palace grounds
rakes along the shore of the North Pond. The palace,
built in the seventeenth century as a home for the retired
emperor Go-Mizuno-o, is no longer extant, but the
extensive gardens remain.

A checkerboard of moss and old temple paving stones, reused in accordance with the spirit of Zen, comprises one part of the so-named "Garden of Eight Phases" that surrounds the main hall of Tofuku-ji Temple. It is the creation of the renowned twentieth-century garden designer Mirei Shigemori.

In the naturalistic setting of Shugaku-in Imperial Villa in the foothills of Mount Hiei, rice fields are still cultivated, as they have been since the retreat was built in the seventeenth century.

A stone representing Amida Buddha stands in a raked gravel garden at Daisen-in Temple. A reed *sudare* blind, hanging from the temple eaves, creates a gentle composition of light and shadow.

KYOTO
KYOTO
KYOTO

京都×京都×京都

2008年2月6日　第1刷発行

著　者　　ゴラーズ・ヴィルハー
　　　　　シャルロッテ・アンダーソン

発行者　　浦　晋亮

発行所　　IBCパブリッシング株式会社
　　　　　〒162-0804 東京都新宿区中里町29番3号 菱秀神楽坂ビル9F
　　　　　Tel. 03-3513-4511 Fax. 03-3513-4512
　　　　　www.ibcpub.co.jp

デザイン　荒井克紀 (アイアンドアイ)

印刷所　　大日本印刷株式会社

Printed in Japan
ISBN 978-4-925080-96-5